PLAYS FOR PERFORMANCE

*A series designed for
contemporary production and study
Edited by
Nicholas Rudall and Bernard Sahlins*

The Mysteries: Creation

*A New Adaptation
by Bernard Sahlins
of the Medieval Mystery Play*

Ivan R. Dee
CHICAGO

Library of Congress Cataloging-in-Publication Data:
Sahlins, Bernard.
    The mysteries—Creation / a new adaptation by Bernard Sahlins of the medieval mystery play.
        p.   cm. — (Plays for performance)
    Adapted from the 15th century cycle of York mystery plays in a version performed by the National Theater of Great Britain.
        ISBN 1-56663-005-3. — ISBN 1-56663-004-5 (pbk.)
    1. Mysteries and miracle-plays, English—Adaptations.   2. Bible—History of Biblical events—Drama.   I. York plays. II. Title.   III. Title: Creation.   IV. Series.
PR6069.A415M9   1992
822'.914—dc20   92-34051

INTRODUCTION

by Bernard Sahlins and Nicholas Rudall

When Court Theatre in Chicago decided to produce *The Mysteries*, we recognized our debt to the English National Theatre's production of the mid-1980s and its adaptation by Tony Harrison of these medieval texts. This famous London production rescued these plays from being museum pieces, dutifully and often wonderfully performed as costumed, antiquarian artifacts. The driving force behind the National's production was that these plays were done by working people for working people.

In editing this series of Plays for Performance, we have recognized the need for American versions of major classical works. The Mystery plays, even in modern adaptations of their Old English verse, have a decidedly Yorkshire ring to them. That is both natural and desirable for performances in England, but we needed a more accessible American text which retained the alliteration, the rhymes, and the naiveté of the original without indulging in false contemporaneity. That is the intent of this adaptation.

The Production

A number of governing principles will make for a successful production:

3

1. The actors should appear to be ordinary working people in their vocal patterns and costume. There is an elusive question of style here, for while the actor is playing God or Abraham or Joseph, he must *seem* accessible and ordinary. As we were advised by Richard Eyre of the National Theatre, "find beer actors, not champagne actors."

2. The stage settings should reflect a sense of "found objects." For our production, set as it was in urban Chicago, this meant that Lucifer's caldron was a yellow toxic-waste drum, and the Garden of Eden was housed in a cart from the Chicago Park District.

3. The magical feature of the performance of this play is the relationship between the actors and the audience. We used the term "promenade" to describe the fact that our audience danced with the actors, were moved around from scene to scene, and were asked to hold items such as candles or clothes.

4. Music is a key to the whole. The music for *Creation* was created by Larry Schanker and the musicians themselves. It fused original compositions with hymns, blues, folk, and spirituals. The score is available on request.

5. Dance is also key. Dance welcomes the audience and creates thematic transitions from scene to scene.

Production Details

The beauty of the piece is that the production demands invention of design. As long as the fiction of "found objects" (designed by the actors is the fiction) predominates, any working-class settings will work, be they urban or rural.

Here is a listing of some of the principal scenic

and costume devices employed in Court Theatre's production:

We performed in Rockefeller Memorial Chapel, a cathedral-like structure at the University of Chicago. Although we did not enjoy the convenience of a theater, we could exploit the chapel's height and architecture. The space was decorated with construction lights. The audience sat in bleachers or on the floor.

We used two forklifts. God was raised up, dressed in overalls and a hard hat. Lucifer's forklift was garishly decorated with silver wings and Christmas lights which could flash on when needed.

Lucifer "fell" into the toxic-waste caldron which was fitted with a red revolving light in its base.

When God created the world, we used a long piece of blue cloth to create waves. This later turned into a "whale" which blew water through a fire extinguisher.

We raised helium balloons as stars and planets.

Eden consisted of The Tree made from two-by-fours with one lone apple. We unrolled a piece of astroturf with pop-up flowers on it. A large gardener's cart brought in these and other such objects. The cart was covered with wood chips. From beneath this mulch emerged Adam and Eve dressed in body stockings.

Lucifer entered with cast members holding hands as the serpent, gliding through the audience.

When Abel cut the sheep's throat, red streamers fell out. The "sheep" should be large enough for Abel to be dragged out on it. Cain's offerings need to produce smoke on demand.

Noah and his wife beat each other with slapsticks. The "ark" was constructed from pallets upon which some of the audience had been standing. The rudder was Cain's plow. The shape of the ark was defined by seated actors holding open umbrellas.

The dove, following the English production, was created by flapping a single umbrella.

The scene with Abraham and Isaac was performed originally by the butchers' guild. Accordingly, it began with the entrance of actors in aprons, sharpening knives. The "sacrifice" took place on a butcher's table made of one of Noah's pallets.

In the Nativity, Gabriel selects the "maiden mild" by reflecting light upon Mary.

Mary gives birth by creating a child out of carefully folded pieces of cloth. While she performs this gentle and beautiful mime, music plays and she is surrounded by members of the audience holding candles.

The kings wear fairly gaudy cloaks, and their crowns were made of found objects.

The donkey was a sawhorse on wheels.

The knights wore welders' masks and used pruning hooks as swords.

The slaughter of the innocents was accomplished by raising upon the pruning hooks the pieces of cloth that formed the babies. The cloths were stained red and became the cloak that Death wore.

These are some suggestions. But theatrical invention is limited only by the following caveat: there is a fine line to be drawn between gimmickry and invention. *Creation* can sustain a certain kind of comic invention at first, but as the play progresses it is better to seek simple transformations of objects to tell the story.

The world premiere of the American adaptation of *Creation* was performed at Rockefeller Memorial Chapel at the University of Chicago by Court Theatre on January 16, 1992. The production was directed by Nicholas Rudall and Bernard Sahlins.

CAST

GOD	Matt De Caro
LUCIFER	Johnny Lee Davenport
GABRIEL	William D. King
ADAM / ISAAC	John Schroeder
EVE	Rebecca MacLean
CAIN / JOSEPH	Tom Amandes
ABEL / HEROD'S SON	Kyle Colerider-Krugh
NOAH / HEROD	Rob Riley
NOAH'S WIFE	Kate Buddeke
ABRAHAM	Daniel Mooney
MARY	Tanya White
THREE KINGS	Johnny Lee Davenport, Michael Raimondi, Craig Ricci Shaynak
THREE SHEPHERDS	Tom Higgins, Dan Mooney, Gavin Witt
THE COMPANY	Tom Amandes, Kate Buddeke, Kyle Colerider-Krugh, Liza Cruzat, Johnny Lee Davenport, Matt De Caro, Jacqueline

Edelberg, Tom Higgins, William D. King, John Leovy, Rebecca MacLean, Daniel Mooney, Michael Raimondi, Rob Riley, John Schroeder, Craig Ricci Shaynak, Tanya White, Gavin Witt

THE BAND Michael Bodeen, Brian Gephart, Willy Schwartz (conductor), Jon Spiegel, Miriam Sturm, Nathan Sturm

Mary Griswold and John Paoletti, Scenic and Costume Designers; Stanley Tigerman, Architectural Consultant; Michael Philippi, Lighting Designer; Robert Neuhaus, Sound Designer; Timothy O'Slynne, Choreographer; Larry Schanker, Composer and Musical Director; Tamara Boutcher, Stage Manager

The Mysteries: Creation

The Company, dressed as workmen, greet the audience as they arrive at their places and talk to them. The band on the stage begins to play a dance tune. A large cloth-covered object is upstage center. Several platforms.

BAND LEADER: Lovely ladies, gentle men, peace; and welcome to our play.

(The band continues the dance tune. The actors come together and dance. Several of them remove the cloth from the object in the center to reveal an industrial lift. The lift rises, bearing God aloft. Fanfare.)

GOD: Ego sum alpha et omega
Vita, via, veritas
Primus et Novissimus

(fanfare)

I am gracious and great, God without beginning.
I am maker unmade, all might is in me.
I am life, and the way unto wealth-winning,
I am foremost and first, as *I* bid shall it be.
My blessing, in bliss shall be blending
A haven, from harm to be hiding;
My body in bliss e'er abiding,
Eternal, without any ending.

(Lucifer is discovered, on a platform. The Angel Gabriel, a Seraphim, and a Cherubim stand on the second level, facing God.)

Since I am maker unmade, and most high in might,

11

And ever am I endless, and nought is but I,
I bid build all about me a bliss, to be bright,
Heaven, home to the angels on high.
Nine orders of angels full clear
In that bliss I bid to be here.

(God raises Lucifer as he speaks.)

Of all the mighty I made, most close after me
I make thee, as master and mirror of my might.
I set you high, here by me, blessed for to be.
I name thee now Lucifer as bearer of light.

(the Angels sing)

ANGEL LUCIFER: All the mirth that is made is marked
in me.
The beams of my brilliance are burning so
bright,
And so seemly in sight myself I now see,
Like a lord am I lifted to live in this light.

(Lucifer is lifted higher)

More favored by far than my friends,
I feel me all flawless and fair;
A loved and legitimate heir,
With power to plot my own ends.

GABRIEL: Lord with a lasting love we love thee
alone,
You mightful maker that molded and made us,
And wrought us thus worthily to dwell as thine
own,
Where never feeling of filth may foul us nor
fade us.
All bliss is here building about us.
If we but stay steadfast in thought,
In the worship of him that us wrought,
Of dread need we never more doubt us.

ANGEL LUCIFER: Oh what!
I am favored and fair and figured full fit;
The form of all fairness upon me is fast.
The wealth that I wield I won by my wit.
The blaze of my brightness burns biggest and
    best.
My showing is shimmering and shining,
So greatly to grace have I grown,
I need no annoyance nor moan.
Here never shall pain put me pining.

SERAPHIM: With all the wit that we wield, we
    worship thy will,
Thou, glorious God, that is ground of all grace;
Aye steadfast, song-filled, let us stand still,
Lord, to feel the full favor of thy fair face.
In life that is loyal, and unending,
Though grief seem groundlessly given;
Who e'er with that grief may be driven,
Redeemed is by thy might so mending.

ANGEL LUCIFER: Oh what!
I am worthily worshiped with wisdom indeed;
For in all glorious glee my glittering it gleams.
I am so mightily made my mind must you heed.
I shall abide in this bliss through brightness of
    beams.
Ah! Ah! That I am blinding bright,
Among you blazing so clear,
As Great God himself glistened here.
Of all heaven have I the light.

CHERUBIM: As bliss is a bastion about us;
So long stay we stable in thought
In the worship of Him that us wrought,
Of dread harm need never more doubt us.

ANGEL LUCIFER: Here shall I set myself full seemly
    to sight,

13

Receiving my reverence through right of renown,
Worshiped like him that is highest on height;
Oh what I am perfect and proud....

(God signals. Lucifer starts to plunge.)

Out! Damn! All goes down.
I'm hurled from heaven. In vain I'm calling.
Gone pomp, gone power. Help, I am falling.

(he sees a fiery caldron beneath him)

No! No! Demons! Helpless! How hot it is here.
This is a pit of perdition. Pity my plight.
What comes over me now, once comely and
   clear?
Now am I lightless, alas, that once was light.
Now my brightness is blackened and blear,
My fate is all fire and flaming,
That mocks me with misery maiming.
Blast! I burn, boiling in brimstone and fear.

(Lucifer leaps into the caldron manned by two devils, Ribald and Beelzebub)

Alas! Woe is me now, now is it worse than it was.
Punished for pride. It was only a thought.

FIRST DEVIL: To hell have you brought us.

LUCIFER: Ye lie! Out, Alas!

SECOND DEVIL: This woe hast thou wrought us.

LUCIFER: Ye lie! Ye lie!
   I thought but a thought. For that you torment
   me,
   And sink me in smoke, and fierce fires rent me?

(the two men spin the caldron through the audience as the band plays Lucifer's song)

(all join in, including the angels)

14

SONG: From evil thought to evil act is but a step.
   He made a pact.

   From evil thought to evil act is but a step. He
      made a pact.

   All must take heed of this condition.
   All must be freed of blind ambition.

   From evil thought to evil act is but a step. He
      made a pact.

GOD: These fools from their fairhood in fantasies
   fell,
   Made mock of my might that marked them and
      made them.
   Wicked their works were; in woe shall they
      dwell.
   They are fallen into filth that forever shall fade
      them.

   But all that me worship shall dwell here indeed,
   Therefore yet more of my work now I will;
   Since they are destroyed who did us dread deed;
   Even in my likeness, their love to fulfill,
   Mankind in my mold will I make;

   But first I will muster my might.
   Since earth is vain void and murkness as well,
   The darkness so name I the night;
   For day I bid, LET THERE BE LIGHT!
   Thus the first day do I bless

   (God creates the earth)

   A firmament now will I frame;
   The wetness, the sea I will name,
   In the whirl of waters give birth
   to heaven above; below, earth.
   Thus the second day do I bless.

(God creates plants)

From land all herbs and grass will spring,
And seed bear fruit and flowers bring.
Thus the third day do I bless.

(God creates the heavens)

The sun and moon and stars I place with
    planets in high heaven's space;
The sun for day, the moon for night,
Set to serve the earth with
    greater and lesser light.

Thus the fourth day do I bless, and I see my
    work is good.

(God creates the animals)

Now from the waters fish will I bring,
Set fowls in the firmament flying,
Great whales to swim, beasts, birds to sing,
Going forth and multiplying.
Thus the fifth day do I bless.

Now make we man. Tomorrow will I rest.
Rise up thou earth in blood and bone
In shape of man, I command thee.

(Adam rises)

A female shall you have to fear;
From thy left rib her life I make.

(Eve rises)

Abiding with you ever here,
Ne'er to leave you, ne'er forsake.
Take now here the ghost of life,
And receive both your souls of me;
This female take thou to thy wife.
Adam and Eve thy names shall be.

Adam and Eve, this peaceful place
To you is granted of my grace
To have your dwelling in.
Herbs, spice, fruit on tree,
Beasts, fowls, all that ye see
Shall bow to you therein.
It is called Paradise.
Here shall your joys begin.

ADAM: Ah, Lord, full mighty is thy might,
And that is seen on every side;
For now is here a joyful sight,
To see this world so long and wide.
Many diverse things here now there is
Of beasts and fowls both wild and tame,
Yet none is made to thy likeness
But we alone. Ah, loved be thy name.

EVE: Loving be lasting to such Lord,
Who us has given so great reward,
To govern both great and small,
And made us after his own thought,
And us such play and pleasure brought
Among these mirths all.
Here is a joyful sight
Where we shall in peace abide.
We love thee, most of might,
Great God, that doth provide.

GOD: Love my name with good intent
And hark to this commandment:
My bidding both obey;
All the fruit that here find ye
Take you thereof full and free
And make you right merry,
But this one tree alone,
Adam, I forbid this,
The fruit of it eat none,
Or be brought out of bliss.

ADAM: Alas! Lord, that we should do so ill.
Thy blessed bidding we shall fulfill,
Both in thought and in deed.
We'll go not near this tree or bough,
Nor taste the fruit that on it grow,
Therewith our flesh to feed.

EVE: We shall do thy bidding;
We have no other need.
The fruit full still shall hang,
Lord, that thou hast forbid.

GOD: Here shall you lead your life
With dainties that is dear.
Adam, and Eve thy wife,
My blessing have you here.

(Exit God and Angels. Enter Satan.)

LUCIFER: My wits are in a whirl with woe.
How, Lucifer, lie thou so low
That lately sat so close to God?
Now pent up and with pitchforks prod;
The brightest angel I ere this,
That ever was or to now is.
The beast of pride betrayed my bliss.
Now man is master. I ask this:
Should such a creature made of clay
Have such a bliss? Him I'll betray.
God to him a mate did send,
In worm's likeness will I wend
And feign for her a likely lie.
Eve! Eve!

EVE: Who is there?

LUCIFER: I, a friend.
Come here to do you favor.
Of all the fruit in paradise
Which may you not savor?

EVE: We may of them each one,
   Fill all need without fear,
   Save for one tree alone,
   Which harms to hie too near.

LUCIFER: And why that tree, that seems, I swear, as
   any tree nearby?

EVE: For Our Lord God forbid us there,
   The fruit of it, Adam nor I
   To come it near;
   And if we did we both should die,
   He said, and cease our solace here.

LUCIFER: Ah, Eve, to my intent
   Take heed, and thou shall hear
   What that same matter meant,
   That filled you with such fear.
   Forbidding that fair fruit to you,
   I know full well that is his skill,
   Because he would none other knew
   What treasure's there to take one's fill.
   For wilt thou see,
   Who eats the fruit of good and ill
   Shall have all knowing well as he?

EVE: What kind of thing art thou,
   That tells this tale to me?

LUCIFER: A worm that knows well how
   That ye may worshiped be.

EVE: What worship should we win thereby
   To eat thereof as needs it nought?
   Our Lord we have makes mastery
   O'er all things that in earth are wrought.

LUCIFER: Woman! Give way!
   To greater state you may be brought,
   If ye will do as I shall say.

19

EVE: To do that are we loth,
Our God so to mispay.

LUCIFER: Nay, no harm for ye both;
Eat it safely ye may,
For peril there none in it lies
But worship and a great delight;
For just as God ye shall be wise,
And peer to him in all his might.
Aye, great Gods shall ye be,
Of ill and good to have knowing,
For to be all wise as he.

EVE: Is this so as thou say?

LUCIFER: Yea; why trust thou not me?
I would in no kind of way
Tell nought but truth to thee.

EVE: Then will I to thy teaching trust,
And take this fruit unto our food.

(she takes the apple)

LUCIFER: Bite on boldly, be not abashed.
Give Adam some, to amend his mood,
Increase his bliss.

(Lucifer withdraws)

EVE: Adam, have here of fruit full good.

ADAM: Alas! Woman, why took you this?
Our Lord commanded us both
To tend this tree of his.
Thy work will make him wroth;
Alas! thou hast done amiss.

EVE: Nay, Adam, grieve thee not yet so,
And I shall say thee reason why;
A worm has given me to know;
We shall be as Gods, thou and I,

If that we eat
Here of this tree; Adam, thereby
Fail thee not this worship to get.
For we shall be as wise
As God that is so great
And gain as great a prize;
Therefore eat of this meat.

ADAM: To eat it I would not refuse,
Should I be sure in thy saying.

EVE: Bite on boldly, for it is true;
We shall, as Gods, know everything.

ADAM: To win that name
I shall taste it at thy teaching.

(he takes the apple and eats)

Alas what have I done, for shame!
Ill counsel. Woe waste thee.
Ah, Eve, thou art to blame;
To this enticed thou me.
My body is my shame!
For I am naked now, I think.

EVE: Alas, Adam, right so am I.

ADAM: And for sorrow sore might we not sink?
For we have grieved God almighty
That made me man:
Broken his bidding bitterly,
Alas that ever we it began.
This work, Eve, hast thou wrought,
And made this bad bargain.

EVE: Nay, Adam, blame me not.

ADAM: Have done! Eve, why whom then?

EVE: The worm to blame were worthy more;
With tales untrue he me betrayed.

21

ADAM: Alas, I listened to thy lore,
  I trusted untruths thou me sayest.
  So may I plead,
  That did it I in bitter haste.
  Could I but ban that dreary deed.
  Our shapes with shame me grieves.
  Wherewith shall they be hid?

EVE: Let us take these fig leaves,
  For what we did, we did.

ADAM: Right, as thou says, so shall it be,
  For we are naked and all bare.
  Fully greatly glad would I hide me
  From my Lord's sight, would I knew where,
  Just anywhere....

GOD: Adam! Adam!

ADAM: Lord!

GOD: Where art thou, there?

ADAM: I hear thee, Lord, and see thee not.

GOD: Say to whom the blame belong,
  This deed, what hast thou wrought?

ADAM: Lord, Eve made me do wrong,
  And to me trouble brought.

GOD: Say, Eve, why hast thou made thy mate
  Eat fruit I bade thee should hang still,
  And commanded none of it to take?

EVE: A worm, my Lord, enticed my will.
  Alas! Alas!
  That ever I did deed so ill!

GOD: Oh, wicked worm! woe wither thee!
  That thou in such a way
  Didst dupe them wickedly.
  My curse then cast I here,

With all the might I may,
And on thy belly shalt thou glide
Forever, full of enmity
To all mankind on every side,
And dirt it shall thy sustenance be
To eat and drink.
Adam and Eve, also ye
In dirt now shall ye sweat and stink,
And travail for your food.

ADAM: Alas, our heaven lost,
We that had all the world's good,
Now pay a grievous cost.

GOD: Now Cherubim, my angel bright,
To middle-earth, swiftly drive these two.

ANGEL: All ready, Lord, as it is right,
Since thy will is that it be so
And thy command:
Adam and Eve, set you to go,
For here may ye no longer stand.
Go quickly forth. Thy fare:
Of sorrow shall ye sing.

ADAM: Alas, with shame and sorrow sad,
My heart heavy, my hands I wring.
I mourn. I am amazed and mad.
Think, heart, the happiness I had
And now have none;
On ground shall I go never glad;
My games are gone.

CAIN AND ABEL

At another part of the theatre a shepherd's dance starts up. A Boy comes forward.

BOY: Hail, all hail! And stop your noise,
Make way, make way for Adam's boys.
Cain with plough, Abel with sheep;
Now mark how well God's law they keep.

(Cain enters, ploughing. Abel enters with a sheep.)

ABEL: God, as he both may and can,
Speed thee, brother, and thy span.

CAIN: Come blow my black, hollow ass.
Then graze your sheep on distant grass.
You're welcome to go far away
And kiss the devil's bum;
Come near and either drive or steer,
But best, go from whence ye come.

ABEL: Brother, there is no one here
That wants thee any woe,
But, dear brother, hear my saw:
It is the custom of our law,
That all who live, if they are wise,
Shall worship God with sacrifice.
Therefore, brother, let us away
To worship God, without delay.

CAIN: Oh what! Send you geese to the fox to
preach?
To the devil your vain sermon's teach.

Shall I leave my plough and everything,
And go with thee to make offering?
Nay, thou findest me not so mad.
Go to the devil, and say too bad.
What gives God to thee to praise him so?
To me he gives but sorrow and woe.

ABEL: Cain, leave this vain carping,
For God gives thee thy living.

CAIN: Yet borrowed I never a penny
Of him—here is my hand!

ABEL: Brother as our elders did us raise;
A tenth of our goods then in this blaze
Burn we, with our own hand, in God's praise.

(Abel with a sheep. Cain with a pile of corn.)

CAIN: May my good fortune visit thee brother;
Each year I find worse than the other.
When all men's corn was fair in field,
Then did mine not one ear yield.
Since he gave me none of his,
No more will I give him of this.

ABEL: Brother, go we forth together;
Blessed be God, we have fair weather.

CAIN: Lay down thy bundle upon this hill.

ABEL: Forsooth, brother, so I will.
God of heaven, honor we.

CAIN: Thou offer first, since mad thou be.

ABEL: God, who shaped the earth and sea,
I pray to thee thou hear my plea,
And take in thanks, if thy will be,
The tithe I offer here to thee;
For I give it in good intent
To thee, My Lord, that all has sent.

I burn it now with steadfast thought,
In worship of him that all has wrought.

(Abel's tithes burn brightly)

CAIN: It is full sore against my will
    To tithe this crop that I did till.
    But now will I take my turn,
    Since I must needs my tenth to burn.

(counting his sheaves; he holds back the best)

One sheaf, one, and this makes two.
But neither of these may I give you.
Two, two, now this is three;
Yes, this also will stay with me.
For myself the best I keep—
I call that thrift—of all this heap....
On! On! Yes! Yes! Four! Lo, here!

(he has chosen a very small sheaf)

Better grew I none this year.
At springtime I sowed good corn,
Yet was it such when it was shorn—
Thistles and briars, yea, plenty—
And every kind of weed that be.
Four sheaves, four. Lo, this makes five:
Keep this up and I'll never thrive!
Five and six; now this is seven—
But never this to God in heaven.
Nor none of these four, I would fight
To keep them from the Good Lord's sight.
Seven ... seven, now this is eight.

ABEL: Cain, come not to God in impious state.

CAIN: Therefore is it that I say,
    I will not deal my goods away.
    We! eight and nine and ten is this;
    We! this may we best miss.

27

(choosing the smallest sheaf)

Give him this and no more;
It goes against my heart full sore.

ABEL: Cain! A tenth of all, I mean.

CAIN: Lo! twelve, fifteen, and sixteen...

(closes his eyes, finishes counting, then reopens them)

Lo, I gave myself a blessing;
I tithed wondrous well by guessing.
And so even—all in line,
Now will I set fire to mine.

(Cain's offering refuses to burn)

Damn! Help me, give it air.
It will not burn for me, I swear.
Puff, this smoke does me much shame.
Now burn, in the devil's name.
Oh! Some devil of hell, I say,
Almost took my breath away.
Had I blown one more breath
I had been choked to death.

ABEL: Cain, thy offering is a joke,
Thy tithe should burn without this smoke.

CAIN: Come kiss the devil in the ass!
Because of thee it burns like glass.
I would gladly stuff thy snout,
With fire, sheaves, and every sprout.

(God appears above)

GOD: Cain, why do you so wrong rebel
Against thy brother Abel?
No need to chide or draw thy sword,
Tithe right and thou gets thy reward.
And be thou sure, if thou tithe untrue,
Thou shalt be paid with what is due.

28

(God withdraws)

CAIN: Why, what was that squeak over the wall!
  Some little elf that piped so small?
  Come, go we hence, from perils all.
  God is out of his wit!
  Come Abel, and our way wend.
  Methink that God is not my friend.
  From here then will I flit.

ABEL: Cain, brother, that is not right.

CAIN: Damn it! why burned your tithe so bright,
  Where mine only smoked
  So fierce it could have both us choked?

ABEL: God's will it is to show your shame.
  If thy tithe smoked, am I to blame?

CAIN: Damn it! For that shall thou sorely pay!
  With cheekbone, ere another day
  Shall I have torn thy life away.

(Strikes Abel with a bone. Abel falls.)

So lie down there and take thy rest.
Thus shall villains be chastised best.

ABEL: Vengeance, vengeance, Lord, I cry;
  Guilt have I none and yet I die.

(dies)

CAIN: Yes, lie there villain! Lie there, lie.

(menaces the audience)

And if any of you think I did amiss,
I, to you, can do far worse than this.

(God appears above)

GOD: Cain! Cain!

CAIN: Who is it that calls me?
I am here. Canst thou not see?

GOD: Cain, where is thy brother Abel?

CAIN: Why ask thou me? I think in hell,
In hell I'm sure he be—
Anyone there I'm sure can see—
Or somewhere he lieth, sleeping;
When was he in my keeping?

GOD: From earth to heaven like a flood,
The voice of thy brother's blood,
That thou has slain, for vengeance cries.
Cain, thou art mad. There your brother lies,
Whom thou hast falsely brought to ground.
For this be ye aye accursed found.

(an angel marks Cain)

Now bitter torment thy endless fate;
For death thou'lt vainly plead and wait,
And none shall pity thy outcast state.

CAIN: No matter. I know the way I wend,
As devil's slave, world without end.
If I come safely through that part,
For any man I give not a fart.

(Drags the body off stage. Song.)

NOAH AND HIS WIFE,
THE FLOOD AND ITS WANING

God appears above.

GOD: Since I, God, who so well this world hatl
    wrought;
    Heaven and earth, and humankind from nought
    I see that my people in deed and thought
    Are foully besotted in sin.

NOAH: Now deeply I dread, God will take
    vengeance,
    Sin is so widespread without any repentance.
    For six hundred years odd led I, without
    distance,
    A life near to the dead, filled with great
    grievance,
    Always.
    And now I wax old,
    Sick, sorry, and cold;
    As muck upon mold
    I wither away.

GOD: *(from above)* Me thought I showed man love
    when I made him to be,
    As angels above, like to the Trinity.
    And now in reproof disgraced is he
    On earth; himself to stuff with sins that
    displease me.
    I will destroy therefore both beast, woman and
    man,

All shall perish, less and more. Our bargain may
    they ban,
That ill did do.
On earth is no lament.
But sin without repent.

NOAH: *(prays)* But yet will I cry for mercy and call:
    Noah, thy servant am I, Lord over all!
    Me and my family, that shall with me fall
    Keep from villainy, and bring to thy hall
    In heaven.
    Keep me from sin
    This world within.
    Comely King of us all,
    I pray thee hear my call.

GOD: Therefore this world lo shall I destroy full
    sore
    With floods that shall flow and run with hideous
    roar.
    I have good cause thereto: for man fears me no
    more.
    As I say shall I do; in vengeance, my sword
    before,
    I make end
    To all that now bear life,
    Save Noah and his wife,
    For they cause no strife
    With me, nor me offend.

(God descends)

NOAH: Ah, Benedicte! What art thou thus
    That appeareth as magic to me? Thou art full
    marvelous!
    Tell me, in charity, thy name so gracious.

GOD: My name is of dignity, and also full glorious
    to know:
    I am God most mighty,

One God in Trinity,
Made thee and each man to be;
To love me well thou ought.

Noah, my friend, my command mark, from
    doom thee to save,
A great ship build, an ark, of nail, of board, and
    stave.

Thou wast always a hard worker, as true as steel
    to me,
To my bidding did ye hark; my friendship shall
    save thy family
From death.

In length thy ship should be
Three hundred cubits, charge I thee;
In height even thirty;
Fifty full in breadth.

NOAH: Bless us, Lord, here for charity I crave,
    The better may we steer the ship that shall us
    save.

GOD: Noah, to thee and to thy kin
    My blessing grant I.
    Ye shall wax and multiply
    And fill the earth again,
    When all these floods have passed
    And fully gone away.

(exit God)

NOAH: Lord, homeward to my task as fast as that I
    may,
    My wife, there will I ask what she will now say,
    And I am aghast that there be some fray
    Betwixt us both.
    A peevish woman she,
    For little, oft angry;

If any thing wrong be,
Soon is she wroth.

(Noah crosses to his wife)

Godspeed, dear wife, how fare ye?

WIFE: How now, as I hope to thrive, the worse for
　　seeing thee.
　　It is time thou did arrive, where could thou thus
　　long be?
　　That we be alive, or dead, is the same for thee.
　　While we toil and strain
　　Thou live without pain,
　　Yet for meat and for grain
　　Have we truly need.

NOAH: Wife, we are hard pressed with tidings new.

WIFE: Rumors frighten you always, be they false or
　　true,
　　But thou deserve to be beaten until black and
　　blue.
　　God knows how I'm treated, and that do I rue
　　full ill;
　　Thou dost nought, only complain
　　Of continual pain;
　　Morn to night that refrain.
　　God send thee once thy fill!

(addressing the women in the audience)

We women must harry all bad husbands.
I have one, by Mary, that makes such demands;
If he fret I must tarry, as he commands,
With semblance full sorry and wring both my
　　hands
In dismay.
But yet otherwhile,
What with game and with guile,

34

I shall smite and smile
And him well repay.

NOAH: What! Hold thy tongue, ram shit, or stilled
it shall be.

WIFE: I swear if thou smite, in return I smite thee.

NOAH: We shall try if you're right. Slut, thou shall
see;
(strikes her) Upon the bone shall it bite.

WIFE: Oh! Mary ill smitest thou me.
But I suppose
I shall not owe thee long,
Pay for thy wrong.
Take thee a strong thong
To tie up thy hose! *(strikes him)*

NOAH: Wilt thou so? Mary, here is my blow. *(strikes)*
I give three for two, I swear by God's woe.
(strikes)
And I give them back before I go. *(strikes)*

(to audience)

Her blows are not weak,
As strong is her shriek.
In faith, no such dread sound
On earth can be found.

But I will keep charity, for I have things to do.

WIFE: Here shall no man tarry thee; I pray thee go
to!
Full well may we miss thee, since peace must I
now woo.
To spin will I set me. *(sits down to spin)*

NOAH: Farewell. I go.
But, wife,
Pray for me fervently
Till I come again for thee.

35

WIFE: Even as thou prays for me
And so long should I thrive.

(goes to his shipbuilding location)

NOAH: Now assay will I
My skill at carpentry.
In nomine patris et fili
Et spiritus sancti. Amen.

(workmen appear)

Lo, here the length,
(measuring) Three hundred cubits exactly;
Of breadth, lo, is it fifty;
The height is even thirty
Cubits full strength.

*(Shipwrights enter and build the arks as Noah contin-
ues. He is more hindrance than help; the carpenters
work around him. The ship is finished and Noah goes
on board.)*

NOAH: This ship will never fail, that dare I undertake
I swear.
Windows, doors, as he said;
Three decks, all well made;
Pitch and tar well laid;
This will last and great weight
Will bear.

Come hither quickly, wife, and consider;
Hence must we flee. We all together.
Come, fast!

WIFE: Why, sir, what ails you?
Who is it assails you?
To flee it avails you
If ye be aghast.

NOAH: There's no time to lose. Come to the ship
fast.

WIFE: Noah, go mend thy shoes, the better will they last.

(thunder, lightning, the rain begins)

WIFE: My, the rain has begun, I stay not long dry;
To the ship with a run, therefore will I hie,
For dread that I drown here.

(she rushes aboard)

NOAH: In faith, and for your long tarrying,
Ye shall taste of the whip.

(the wife appeals to the women in the audience)

WIFE: Make me a widow, Lord, answer my needs.
I would be happy, Lord, to wear widow's weeds.
For the good of his soul, Lord, I'd gladly say grace;
So would the others, Lord, I see in this place.
All wives who are here,
For the life that they led,
Wish their husbands were dead.
And I swear by my head,
So wish I my husband were.

(Noah appeals to the men in the audience)

NOAH: Ye men that have wives, whilst they are young,
If you love your own lives, chastise their tongue.

(takes the helm)

Now to the helm am I bent,
And to my ship attend.

WIFE: I see in the firmament,
Me think, the seven planets.

NOAH: This is a great flood, wife, take heed.

WIFE: So me thought as I stood. We are in great
     dread.
     These waves are so wild

NOAH: Help, God, in this need!
     As thou art steersman good, the best, us to lead,
     Of all,
     Thou rule us in this sea,
     As thou hast promised me.

WIFE: In great peril we be.
     Help, God, when we call!

(Song. The storm abates.)

NOAH: Now are the weathers ceased, and the
     cataracts knit,
     Both the most and the least.

WIFE: Methink by my grace,
     The sun shines in the east. Is that not its face?
     We should have a good feast, where those floods
     did race
     In such a wrath.

NOAH: We have been here, all we,
     Three hundred days and fifty.

WIFE: Yea, and now wanes the sea.
     Lord, thou our love hath.

     What ground may this be?

NOAH: The hills of Armenie,

(he releases a dove)

     Where now will I release
     A true dove of peace.
     With flight of wing
     Bring, without tarrying,
     Of mercy some tokening,
     Either from north or south.

WIFE: Gone but a little, she cometh, lew, lew.
   She brings us in her bill, some tidings new.
   Behold,
   It is of an olive tree
   A branch, thinketh me.

NOAH: So it is, I see.
   Right so it is called.

   Dove, bird, full blessed, fair might thee befall.
   Thou art true to thy tryst as stone in the wall.

WIFE: A true token is't, we shall be saved all.
   Lord, now to me list, no more pain us befall.

NOAH: Go we without shame.
   We need no longer abide here.

   (they disembark)

   Behold, in this greensward not cart nor plow;
   There is left to be seen not tree nor bough;
   Nothing, nothing, all is away;
   Castles, towns, great in their day
   Destroyed....

WIFE: But Noah, where now all our kin
   And company we knew before?

NOAH: Dame, all are drowned, let be thy din,
   Now paid they for their sins full sore.
   Good living let us now begin,
   So that we grieve our God no more.
   This rainbow has he set us then
   As a tokening, between him and us,
   For teaching to all Christian men,
   That since the world was ravaged thus
   With water, would he ne'er waste again.
   Thus has God, most of might,
   Set his sign full clear,

Up in the air so high,
The rainbow in his sky,
As men may see it aye,
In seasons of the year.

ABRAHAM AND ISAAC

Abraham, with his young son Isaac, kneels in prayer.

ABRAHAM: Father of heaven, omnipotent,
In old age thou hast granted me this;
That with me shall dwell this sweet son.
Nothing I love would I so miss
Except thine own self, dear Father of bliss,
As Isaac here, my own loved one.

And therefore, Father of heaven, I thee pray
For his health, and also for his grace.
Now, Lord, keep him both night and day,
That never disease nor harm may
Come to my child in any place.

Now come on, Isaac, my own sweet child;
Go we home and take our rest.

ISAAC: Abraham, my own dear father so mild,
To follow you is to be blessed
Both early and late.

ABRAHAM: Come on, sweet child, I love thee best
Of all the children that ever I begat.

GOD: Abraham, my servant Abraham!

ABRAHAM: Lo, Lord, already here I am.

GOD: Abraham, hear me. It is my will;
Isaac, your loved son, you shall take
And kill him there on yonder hill;
Thus with his blood you sacrifice make.

ABRAHAM: My Lord, it is ever my intent
  To thee to be obedient.
  The son that thou to me has sent,
  Offer I will to thee.
  High Lord, God omnipotent,
  Thy bidding done shall be.

  Make thee ready, my dear darling,
  For we must do a little thing.
  This wood do thou on thy back bring.
  We may no longer wait.

  A sword and fire I will take
  For sacrifice that I must make.
  God's bidding will I not forsake,
  But ever obedient be.

  *(Abraham takes a sword and fire. Isaac takes a bundle
  of sticks and follows his father.)*

ISAAC: I am full ready, my father, dear,
  And whatsoever you bid of me,
  It shall be done with glad cheer,
  For love of thee.

ABRAHAM: O! Lord of Heaven, my hands I wring.
  This child's words do wound deep my heart.

  Now, Isaac, son, go we our way
  Onto yon mount, with all our main.

ISAAC: Go, my dear father, as fast as you may;
  I follow you though it doth pain
  And I be slender.

ABRAHAM: O! Lord, my heart breaketh in twain;
  This child's words, they be so tender.

  (they reach the mountain)

ISAAC: Father, somehow I feel me sore afraid.
  Why make ye thus this heavy cheer?

Both fire and wood we have here laid,
But no beast to kill have I seen here.

ABRAHAM: Dread not, my child, and my word take,
Our Lord will send one to this hill.

ISAAC: Yes, father, but my heart beginneth to quake
To see that sharp sword set to kill.

ABRAHAM: O! Father of heaven such is my woe!
This child here breaketh my heart in two.

ISAAC: Tell me, my dear father, speaketh ye plain;
Your bare sword is drawn for me?

ABRAHAM: O! Isaac, sweet son! Pain! Pain!
For indeed thou break my heart in three.

ISAAC: Dear father, I pray you, hide nothing from
me.
All that you do think you must me tell.

ABRAHAM: Ah! Isaac! Isaac! I must kill thee.

ISAAC: Kill me, father? Alas, is this thy will?
If I have trespassed now, make me mild
With a stick, not with sharp sword kill me now.
Dear father, I am but a child.

ABRAHAM: Forgive me, son. Unless I thee kill
I should grieve God right sore I dread.

ISAAC: And is it God's command, and also his will,
That you should your son's blood shed?

ABRAHAM: Yea, truly, Isaac, my son so good,
Therefore my hands I wring in pain.

ISAAC: Now, father, against my dear Lord's will
I'll never complain, good or ill.
Therefore do what God has bid,
But tell not my mother what you did.

43

ABRAHAM: O! Isaac, Isaac, blessed may thou be.
My heart is faint,
Thy blessed body's blood to see.

ISAAC: *(kneeling)* Father, since it may be no other
way,
Let it come and quickly let it go.
But father, ere death taketh me today,
Pray bless me, for I love you so.

ABRAHAM: Now, Isaac, with all my breath
My blessing I give upon this land;
And surely God will bless your death.
O! Isaac, Isaac, son, up thou stand.

ISAAC: Now farewell, my father. Please, no cries,
And greet my mother with loving word.
But I pray you, father, to hide my eyes,
That I see not the stroke of your sharp sword.

ABRAHAM: Son, thy words make me to weep full
sore.
Now, my dear son, Isaac, speak no more.

ISAAC: O my own dear father, wherefore
And since that I must needs be dead,
Dear father, now to you I pray;
Smite but a few strokes at my head,
And make an end as soon you may.

ABRAHAM: Come up, sweet son, upon mine arm.
Though it do my heart but harm,
I must bind you, hand and foot,
Ere on the altar you are put.

(Abraham binds Isaac)

ISAAC: Indeed sweet father, I am sorry to grieve
you.
I ask you mercy for that I have done,
And for any wrongs I ever did against you.

44

(Abraham lifts Isaac to the altar)

ABRAHAM: Therefore, my dear son, here shall thou
   lie;
Me to my work I must apply.
Surely I would instead gladly die
If God will be pleased with my death.

ISAAC: O, mercy, father, mourn ye no more.
Your weeping maketh my heart sore
As my own death. Please, father, be kind.
Your kerchief about my eyes will ye wind?

(here Abraham lays a cloth over Isaac's face, saying)

ABRAHAM: Now farewell, my child so full of grace.

ISAAC: O, father, father, turn downward my face!

ABRAHAM: *(aside)* To do this deed I am full sorry,
But Lord, thy charge I'll not withstand.

ISAAC: O, Father of heaven, to thee I cry;
Lord, receive me into thy hand.

ABRAHAM: Now heart, why wouldst not thou break
   in three?
Yet thou shall not make me to my God untrue.
I will no more delay for thee,
For unto God I give his due.

*(here Abraham draws his sword and God takes the
sword in his hand suddenly)*

GOD: Abraham, stay. Thy hand hold still.
Slay not thy son. For God doth heed
Your plea. To spare your son is now His will.
Since thou for Him wouldst do this deed.

Thy son is spared, but mark you well,
I shall my own son, without sin,
Sacrifice, to save all from hell

45

The devil has put mankind in.
Thy son I spared, he loves thee still.
Like thine own Isaac, my beloved lad shall do
    great gladly his father's will,
But not be spared strokes sore and sad,
But done to death upon a hill.

ABRAHAM: O, Lord, I thank thee for thy great
    prize;
Now am I comforted by thee.
Arise up, Isaac, my dear son, arise,
Arise up, sweet child and come to me.

THE NATIVITY

The Angel Gabriel appears above.

GABRIEL: Know, Isaiah says a maiden mild
　　Shall bear a son among Hebrews.
　　Of all countries shall he be king,
　　And govern all that on earth grows.
　　Emanuel shall be his name—
　　To say, God's son in heaven.

JOSEPH: I am deceived—by every sign
　　My young wife is with child full great.
　　The child surely is not mine—
　　Though prophecy of old did state,
　　A virgin clean shall bear a child—
　　But surely it cannot be she—
　　Though she be, surely, undefiled.
　　Therefore must I deceived be.
　　Thus I think I must be gone;
　　Of my going will I none warn—
　　But ere I go it is mine intent
　　To ask from whom that child was borne;
　　That would I know before I went.

(enter Mary)

MARY: Welcome as God me speed.
　　Doubtless, to me, he is full dear;
　　Joseph, my spouse, welcome are ye.

JOSEPH: God's mercy, Mary. Say, what cheer?
　　Tell me in truth, how is't with thee?

Who has been there?
Thy womb is grown great, so think me.
Thou art with child, alas! despair.
Whose is't Mary?

MARY: Sir, God's and yours.

JOSEPH: No. No,
I am deceived, I know it plain.
And how know I?
With my flesh, thy flesh hast never lain.
Yet thou art with child. My shame I cry;
For me this is a shameful case;
In vain I rave, my mind's awry,
I dare look no man in the face,
My grief so heavy I would die.
Whose is the child that thou dost bear?

MARY: Yours, sir, and the king's of bliss.

JOSEPH: Thou art young and I am old,
These games I disavow.
In confidence, I must be told;
Whose is the child thou art with now?

MARY: Now great God in his might
Omniscient, cast thy light
As meekly I do bow.
Pity this person's plight
And in his heart alight;
The truth for him to know.

JOSEPH: Who hath thy maidenhead, Mary? Or
don't you know?

MARY: I swear I am a maiden clean.

JOSEPH: Nay, such madness cannot be so,
Such thing no man has seen;
A maiden to be with child!
These words from thee are wild.
It cannot have ever been.

MARY: Joseph, ye are beguiled,
  With sin was I ne'er defiled,
  God's gift is in me seen.

JOSEPH: God's gift? Fah, Mary. God, help!

(Gabriel appears)

GABRIEL: I, Gabriel, God's angel, by his command
  Have taken Mary to my keeping,
  Am sent to thee by God's demand;
  In legal wedlock thou stay thee.
  Leave her not, I forbid thee.
  No sin of her thou reprimand,
  But to her fast thou speed thee.
  Of her no longer doubt thee;
  It is God's word from heaven grand.

  The child that shall be born of her,
  It is conceived of the Holy Ghost.
  All joy and bliss that shall be after,
  And to all mankind of all the most.
  Jesus, his name thou call.
  Such fate shall him befall
  As thou shall see anon.
  His people save he shall
  From evils and trials, all,
  That they to now have born.

JOSEPH: And is this truth, angel, thou says?

GABRIEL: Yea, and this it's sign as right;
  Go forth to Mary, thy wife always,
  Bring her to Bethlehem this very night.
  There shall a child born be,
  God's son of heaven is he,
  And man, ay, of most might.

JOSEPH: My back glad would I bow,
  And ask forgiveness now.

MARY: Forgiveness, sir? Let be, for shame.
   Such word should all good women lack.

JOSEPH: Yea, Mary, I am to blame
   For words before I to thee spake.
   But gather we now all our gear,
   Such worn weeds as we wear,
   And stow them in a sack.
   I will to Bethlehem it bear,
   For little things do women fear;
   Help, up now, on my back.

The stable.

MARY: Now in my soul great joy have I;
   I am clad in comfort clear.

JOSEPH: I would be glad we had some light,
   Whate'er befall.
   It grows so dark unto my sight,
   And cold withal.
   I go find fuel for light.

(he leaves)

*(The birth is managed on stage by means of the virgin
kneeling in prayer to God, then rising and parting her
cloak to reveal the child before her. The birth is seen to
be serene and painless.)*

(Joseph returns)

JOSEPH: Oh, Mary, what sweet thing is that on thy
   knee?

MARY: It is my son, the truth to say,
   That is so good.

JOSEPH: Now welcome, flower, fairest of hue;
I will thee worship, main and might.
Hail, my maker, hail Christ Jesu,
Hail, royal king, root of all right,
Hail, saviour,
Hail, my Lord of life and light,
Hail, blessed flower.

The open fields. Three kings are scanning the sky.

KING 1: Lord, thy fair mercy give
On three kings who pray to know
Whether thou dost on earth live,
That we may to thy dwelling go.

KING 2: Lord, such time as is thy will,
Ancient prophecy to fulfill,
Give us a sign, quick or still,
That will us thy coming show.

KING 1: For when a star with beams bright,
Out of the East will stable stand;
Then will be born a babe that night,
Who will be lord of every land.

(the star appears)

ANGEL: Rise up ye kings three,
And come along after me,
Into the land of Judee.
The child you seek, there shall you see,
Born all of a maiden free;
The king of heaven and earth shall be.

KING 2: Lords, hie we hither then anon.
We are bidden.

(the star vanishes)

KING 3: Alas, where has the star gone?
Of its last light is there none.
Which is our way?

(enter Messenger)

Say, friend, that rides by there,
Tell us some tidings, if ye may.

MESSENGER: What is your will, sir?

KING 1: Can you say what place, or where,
A child is born who the crown will bear,
And of the Jews be king?

MESSENGER: Let me warn you, sir, I pray,
If King Herod heard you so say,
He would go mad this very day,
And fly out of his skin.

KING 1: What is this Herod that would so
Rant and rave against a child?

MESSENGER: A king, that would bring grievous woe
To you who utter words so wild.

KING 2: Sir, since there is a king so near,
Let us duly greet our fellow peer.
And ask his leave through his realm to pass.
And travel safe therein.

MESSENGER: The palace lies this way from here,
Wherein he does dwell.
But if he knew what you say here—
That one is born with great power,
You would be in great danger—
Such a thing to tell.

(exit Messenger)

KING 1: We journey forth to see this king,
Whom I have heard is knave most wild;

His leave to ask. But trust nothing.
He would but harm the child.

The fields.

SHEPHERD 1: We wretched chattel that farm on the
    moor,
Living like cattle, our homes are so poor.
No wonder, as it stands, we are not secure;
For the soil of our lands lies fallow and poor.

SHEPHERD 2: As you know,
We are so abused;
Thrice taxed, and confused,
We are badly ill used
By these gentry men.
But the most harried, wherever we go,
Are we who are married, we have the most woe.

(to the audience)

Ye young men, of wooing, fore God, think you
    twice.
Be well wary of wedding, for you pay a price.
"Had I known" is a thing that sounds very nice,
But you'll be in mourning for this terrible vice.
Wives cackle,
Then begin they to croak,
To groan and to cluck,
Like a hen or a cock,
And you they shall shackle.

(First Shepherd tries to whistle to get his attention)

For as sure as you were born, your wife you will
    fear,

Her hand in your purse, her expression a sneer.
Mine has brows like a bristle and a sour face to
　　cheer;
And once she wets her whistle she can sing full
　　clear
Her paternoster.
She's as great—as a whale,
And most hearty and hale,
But by my cup of ale,
I would to God I lost her.

(the First Shepherd interrupts him)

SHEPHERD 1: *(to audience)* God help you people.
(to Second Shepherd) Canst thou be such a bore?

SHEPHERD 2: I could say much more.

(Third Shepherd enters, excited)

SHEPHERD 3: Brethren, in haste take heed and
　　hear
What I will speak and specify;
That a prince without a peer,
Our forefathers did prophecy
Would in Bethlehem appear;
That a babe would there be born
So all mankind might unify,
Be healed, those that are lorn.

SHEPHERD 2: Ere he be born, I have heard say,
A star would shine and signify
With lightful gleams, like any day.

SHEPHERD 3: That star, I swear, I have seen!

(Angels appear)

Oh! Hey!

SHEPHERD 1: Oh my God!

SHEPHERD 2: Listen to me!

SHEPHERD 3: *(he has not yet seen the Angels)* What madness comes on thee?

SHEPHERD 1: Step over here and stand on my right,
And tell me truly then,
If you ever saw such a sight!

SHEPHERD 3: I? No, nor surely any other man.

ANGEL: Hark, herdsmen mild; thy glad carols sound.
Now is born a fair child to bind up thy wound,
Take from thee that wild beast that Adam
    unbound.
God on thee has smiled here on this ground.
That you shall know
To Bethlehem go, sure,
Where lieth he, pure
In a crib so poor
Between two beasts
In a manger low.

(the Angels withdraw)

SHEPHERD 1: So exquisite a sound did me so mystify,
I was scared and spellbound by this voice from
on high.

SHEPHERD 2: God's son is now found. This song
    filled the sky,
And the woods all around seemed alight to the
eye.
We must go.

SHEPHERD 3: To Bethlehem fair.

SHEPHERD 1: To seek a child there.

SHEPHERD 2: *(points)* Yon star tells us where
His glory doth show.

(they go to Bethlehem)

Herod's court. Herod's son appears and addresses the audience.

SON: My Father, Herod, that kind king, by
    Mahomet's grace,
Stern sovereign of Jewry, that wandering race,
To you, that are present here on this ground,
Gives gracious greeting, commands you be bound
By his bidding.
Love him with loyalty;
Dread his stern royalty;
Serve him at his pleasure
Humbly, to his measure.

(confidential) Though exceedingly kind
He is strangely sad.
A boy preys on his mind,
Born to be bad.
A king, they him call and that we deny;
That this should befall, great wonder have I.
Therefore, overall, shall I give this cry.
(as if reading an edict) You talk of no king...
But Herod. Ye dread
That lord. His praises sing—
Or lose your head.

(enter Herod accompanied by Knights)

HEROD: The clouds clapped in clearness that these
    climates enclose—
Jupiter and Jove, Mars and Mercury amid—
Racing over my realm to win my rejoicing,
Bidding their blasts to blow when I bid—
Saturn my subject that subtly is hid,

56

Waits on my wanting and lays him full low.
Then clouds from the red sky I rapidly rid,
Thunderbolts terrible by thousands I throw,
As I choose.
Venus her vows to me owes,
And princes pursue as I wish.

Lords and ladies, my virtues behold,
For I am fairest of face and grandest of guise.
How think ye these tales that I told?
I am worthy, witty, and wise.
My son that is seemly, and is such like his sire,
He's learned in Latin, and all him admire.
I'm bold, the blood-shedder, my boy has the
    brains.

SON: All hail, pater, most potent, who right royally
    reigns
And beats back the rebels with blows from his
    blade.

HEROD: Hail, lad, my adviser, my consort and aide.
Come close to thy father and clasp thou his
hand.

(they shake hands)

SON: He's mighty in muscle.

HEROD: He's mighty in mind.

BOTH: Betwixt and between us we master mankind.

SON: He rules and wields power.

HEROD: He can read, he can write. With his mind ...

SON: ... and his muscle ...

BOTH: ... we maintain our might.

HEROD: All those against us get defeated and done
By the bruising ...

SON: ...and brainy...

HEROD: ...Herod...

SON: ...and son.

(enter Messenger)

MESSENGER: My Lord, sir Herod, king with crown.

HEROD: Peace, dastard in the devil's fury.

MESSENGER: Sir, a grave event is in this town.

HEROD: What, harlot! Wish ye injury?
Go beat yon boy and knock him down.

SON: Father, this dastard leave to me,
He dare to thee speak so. For shame.

MESSENGER: Lord, messengers should no man blame;
It may be for your own far fame.

HEROD: Then I would hear; tell on then, right.

MESSENGER: My lord, I met at morn,
Three kings talking together
Of He that is now born;
And they hope to come hither.

HEROD: Three kings! in truth?

MESSENGER: Sir, so I say,
For I saw them myself all clear.

SON: My father, torture him, I say.

HEROD: Say fellow, are they far or near?

MESSENGER: My lord, they will be here this day.
That say I sure. No doubt is there.

HEROD: Have done. Dress us in rich array,
And every man make merry cheer,
That no semblance be seen

But friendship fair and still,
Till we learn where they lean,
Whether it be good or ill.

(enter Three Kings)

KING 1: The lord that lends this lasting light
Which has led us out of our land,
Keep thee, sir, king and comely knight,
And all the folk that do here stand.

HEROD: Mahomet, my God, and most of might,
That has my health all in his hand,
Keep thee, sir, king and comely knight,
And tell us now your new errand.

KING 1: In sum we say you, sir,
A star rose ere morn
That made us then inquire
Of one that is newborn.

HEROD: This were a wondrous thing.
Say what babe should that be?

KING 2: Sir, he shall be king
Of Jews and of Jewry.

HEROD: King! In the devil's way, dogs, fie!
Now I see well ye rage and rave,
At any shimmering in the sky.
Ye should know which is king, which knave.
Nay, I am king and none but I;
That shall you know, in case ye crave.
And I am judge of all Jewry;
To speak or spoil, to say or save.
Your tricks may greatly grieve,
And witness what never was.

KING 3: Lord we ask nought but leave,
By your power, to pass.

HEROD: Wither? In the devil's name,
   To seek a lad here in my lands?
   False harlots, return from whence ye came;
   Ye shall be beaten, bound with iron bands.

SON: *(aside)* Father, ye need not be abased.
   This battle may to end be brought.
   Bid them go forth and friendly taste
   The truth of this that they have sought,
   And tell it you; so you may test
   Whether this tale be true or nought.
   Then shall we strike and them arrest,
   And useless make what they have wrought.

HEROD: *(aside)* Well said, thou art thy father's son.
   This answer pleases me.

   Sir Kings, thy wish is won.
   Go forth thy lad to see.
   And come again when you have done
   And tell me how he truly be;
   And if he is a holy one,
   Him will I honor as do ye.

KING 1: Sure, sir, we shall you say
   All the news of that son,
   In all the haste we may.

SON: Farewell. Have a nice day.

   (the Kings exit)

HEROD: By Mahomet, come they again
   All three traitors shall be slain,
   And that same swaddling swain
   I shall chop off his head.

   (Herod and Son laugh together)

The stable.

SHEPHERD 1: Hail, comely and clean, hail, young
child!
Hail, our maker, unseen, of a maiden so mild.
Thou hast vanquished that mean devil so wild.
That beguiler so keen, himself is beguiled.
Lo, he's merry (of Christ),
Lo, he laughs, my sweet thing.
A very fine meeting!
I promised this greeting.
Here a cluster of cherries.

SHEPHERD 2: Hail, full of favor that made all of
nought.
Hail! I kneel and I cower. A bird have I brought
Thee, after
Hail, tiny heart;
Of our creed, first thou art.
From thee all things start,
Little day star.

SHEPHERD 3: Hail, sweet is thy cheer. My heart
doth bleed
To see thee lie here in so poor a bed,
With no pennies.
Hail! Let thy hand fall,
I bring thee but a ball
To have and play thee withal
And go to the tennis.

MARY: Our father supreme, God omnipotent,
Who in his great scheme, his son he has sent,

Called my name in a dream, then gleamed ere
    he went.
I conceived him in esteem, of God's might, as he
    meant.
And now is he born.
May he keep you from woe!
I shall pray him so
Tell all as you go
And remember this morn.

SHEPHERD 1: Farewell, lady, so fair to behold,
    With thy child on thy knee.

SHEPHERD 2: But he lies full cold. *(covers him with*
    sheepskin)
    Lord, well is me! Now we go, thou behold.

(they go out)

SHEPHERD 1: As the prophets foretold, this babe
    have we seen.
    Let us stay, him to guard,
    From harm him to hold.

(the Three Kings enter)

KING 1: Woe to Herod,
    That cursed knight.
    Woe to that tyrant night and day.
    Of our star, through him, we have lost sight.

(the Three Kings kneel and pray)

KING 2: Thou child, whose might no tongue may
    tell,
    As thou art Lord of heaven and hell;
    Thy noble star, Emanuel,
    Thou send us here;
    That we may know by wood and dell
    How we shall fare.

(the star reappears)

KING 3: Ah sirs! I see it stand
　　Above where he is born.
　　Lo, here is the house at hand.
　　We have not missed this morn.

SHEPHERD 1: Whom seek ye, sirs, by ways so wild,
　　With talking, traveling to and fro?
　　Here dwells a woman with her child
　　And her husband; 'tis only so.

KING 2: We seek a child that all shall shield;
　　His certain sign has said us so;
　　And his mother, a maiden mild.
　　Here hope we now to find those two.

SHEPHERD 1: Behold here, sirs, and see
　　Your way to an end is brought.

(they kneel to the Christ Child)

KING 1: Hail be thou, maker of every thing,
　　That weal from all our woes may bring!
　　In token that thou art our king,
　　And shall be ay,
　　Receive this gold as my offering,
　　Prince, I thee pray.

KING 2: Hail, conqueror of king and of knight,
　　That formed fish and fowl in flight!
　　And all ruling;
　　I bring thee incense, as is right,
　　Thus my offering.

KING 3: Hail, king so mild, on mother's knee!
　　Hail, single God in persons three!
　　In token that thou dead shall be,
　　As one of us,
　　For thy burying, this myrrh of me,
　　Receive thee thus.

MARY: Sir Kings, my blessings be with you
  Whereso ye dwell.

(the Kings leave the stable)

Herod's court.

HEROD: The devil!
  Why are those kings not here?
  They promised to appear
  With tidings for my ear.

SON: Father, the kings have gone,
  Each to his own country.

HEROD: What! Fie, rascals, louts, and liars every
    one,
  Traitors. Hell's fires. Knaves, but knights none.

SON: Sir, more of their meaning
  Yet well I understood;
  How they made offering
  Unto that child so good
  That was so newly born.
  They say he should be king.

HEROD: By my life and limb,
  I shall that false king slay.
  My plan it is but dim
  On what to do this day.

SON: Lord, gather in great rout
  Your knights so sharp to strike,
  And search in every stead
  All boy babes all about;
  And leave them dead.

64

HEROD: Yes! That is well said
  Sir Knights, . . .

SON: Ah, now shall we see.

HEROD: To Beth'lem must ye wend,
  With shame to make his end
  That means to master me.
  Lurk there till he be caught
  And let me tell you how:
  Because you know him not,
  All boys under two, now
  To death must they be brought.

The Angel Gabriel appears to Mary and Joseph.

GABRIEL: Hear me, Joseph, and without fear;
  My saying will save thee sorrows sore.
  Be not troubled, help is here;
  In this place canst thou stay no more.

JOSEPH: But what art thou with warning shrill
  Thus in this place that speaks to me?
  To me appear,
  And let me hear
  What that thou wish.

GABRIEL: Joseph, have thou no dread,
  Thou shalt know ere I pass;
  Therefore to me take heed,
  Gabriel, God's angel bright;
  I come to bid thee flee
  With Mary and your son, tonight;
  For Herod the King doth death demand
  For all boy children in the land.

Now then go you
With your dear two,
Till danger be away.
In Egypt shall ye stay,
The Lord's will ye shall obey.

(Mary, Jesus, and Joseph begin their journey)

(Joseph and Mary on a donkey holding the baby Jesus meet a group of mothers with babies. They go on, leaving the mothers behind.)

SOLDIER 1: *(offstage)* Come forth, fellows, appear.
Lo, foundlings find we here.

(The soldiers surround the women. They murder their babies.)

WOMAN 1: Monstrous villains, I cry!
Ye slay my seemly son.

WOMAN 2: Alas, this loathsome strife!
No bliss will I more get,
This knight upon his knife,
Has slain my son so sweet.

WOMAN 1: Alas, that we were wrought
In world, women to be.
The sons that we dear bought
Thus in our sight to see,
Are now all sleeping.

Herod and Son and Knights at banquet.

KNIGHT 1: Lord, as you bade us we have done.

HEROD: I ask but after one,
The kings told of before.

66

KNIGHT 2: Lord, they are dead, every one.
What would ye we did more?

HEROD: Then, sir, by sun and moon,
You are welcome home,

There is no lord alive worth a bit next to me.
My thanks, gentle knights, I owe much to thee.
High time now me thinketh at dinner we were.
Therefore set a table with rich, worthy fare.

(he bids them sit at a table)

SOLDIER 1: Lord, at your bidding we take our seat.
With hearty will obey we thee.
There is no lord of might so great
Through all the world, in no country,
In such honor to dwell.

HEROD: I was never merrier on any morn
Since the day I was born
Than I am now, right on this morn.
Indeed my joy doth swell!

(Death comes forward while the banquet continues)

DEATH: Oh! I heard a man praising pure pride,
All princes in power he surpasses thinks he.
He deems himself worthiest of all this world
wide.
King over all kings that churl wants but to be.
He went into Beth'lem to seek on every side
Christ for to kill, if him they did see.
But his wicked will, the lout, was set aside!
God's son doth live; there is no Lord but he;
Over all lords he is king.
I am Death, God's messenger.
Almighty God hath sent me here
Yon lout to slay, never fear,
For his wicked workings.

HEROD: Spare not wine nor bread,
  For now am I king alone.
  As worthy as I be, there be none.
  Therefore, knights, be merry each one,
  For now my foe is dead.

SOLDIER 1: When those boys sprawled at my spear's
    tip,
  By Satan, our sire, it was a goodly sight!
  A good game it was that boy for to rip,
  Who would have been our king and put you
    from your right.

HEROD: All those bodies about!
  He is dead, I have no doubt.
  Therefore, minstrels, round about,
  Blow a merry strain!

DEATH: I am sent from God; Death is my name.

  *(here, while they sound the trumpet, Death kills Herod
  and the soldiers)*

  (Satan appears)

SATAN: All over, all over! This chattel is mine.
  I shall them bring into my cell.
  I shall teach them games fine,
  And show them such mirth as is in hell.
  They shall envy the swine
  That evermore stink. There shall they dwell.
  (he addresses his victims) With you I go my way.
  I bring you from here with me
  And show you our kind of glee,
  Our mirths now you shall see,
  And ever sing, "welaway."

  (he leads them to hell)

  *The band plays. Mary and Joseph enter with the child.
  The townspeople, carrying lanterns, surround the holy
  family. The Family walks off as the people sing a
  Hosannah.*

ELEPHANT PAPERBACKS

Theatre and Drama

Robert Brustein, *Reimagining American Theatre*, EL410
Robert Brustein, *The Theatre of Revolt*, EL407
Irina and Igor Levin, *Working on the Play and the Role*, EL411
Plays for Performance:
    Aristophanes, *Lysistrata*, EL405
    Anton Chekhov, *The Seagull*, EL407
    Georges Feydeau, *Paradise Hotel*, EL403
    Henrik Ibsen, *Ghosts*, EL401
    Henrik Ibsen, *Hedda Gabler*, EL413
    Henrik Ibsen, *When We Dead Awaken*, EL408
    Heinrich von Kleist, *The Prince of Homburg*, EL402
    Christopher Marlowe, *Doctor Faustus*, EL404
    The Mysteries: Creation, EL412
    August Strindberg, *The Father*, EL406

Literature and Letters

Stephen Vincent Benét, *John Brown's Body*, EL10
Philip Callow, *Son and Lover: The Young D. H. Lawrence*, EL14
James Gould Cozzens, *Castaway*, EL6
James Gould Cozzens, *Men and Brethren*, EL3
Clarence Darrow, *Verdicts Out of Court*, EL2
Floyd Dell, *Intellectual Vagabondage*, EL13
Theodore Dreiser, *Best Short Stories*, EL1
Joseph Epstein, *Ambition*, EL7
André Gide, *Madeleine*, EL8
John Gross, *The Rise and Fall of the Man of Letters*, EL18
Irving Howe, *William Faulkner*, EL15
Aldous Huxley, *Ape and Essence*, EL19
Aldous Huxley, *Collected Short Stories*, EL17
Sinclair Lewis, *Selected Short Stories*, EL9
William L. O'Neill, ed., *Echoes of Revolt: The Masses,*
    1911–1917, EL5
Ramón J. Sender, *Seven Red Sundays*, EL11
Wilfrid Sheed, *Office Politics*, EL4
Tess Slesinger, *On Being Told That Her Second Husband Has*
    Taken His First Lover, and Other Stories, EL12
Thomas Wolfe, *The Hills Beyond*, EL16